HOW TO CONQUER NEGATIVE SELF-TALK

A guided journal for men and women to improve self-esteem and attain personal goals.

Natasha Attard Ph.D.

To my two remarkable boys, Giovanni and Beppe,

This book is dedicated to you with all my love and gratitude. Our endless discussions on the intricacies of the mind, the transformative power of positivity, the strategies to conquer negative self-talk, and the profound impact of mindfulness have been a constant source of inspiration.

May this dedication serve as a testament to our shared journey of discovery and growth. Your presence in my life has enriched it in countless ways, and I hope that the lessons within these pages will also enrich the lives of those who read them.

With all my love,
Mom

Contents

Introduction

Dear reader,

Welcome to an exploration of self-discovery and empowerment. The path we're embarking upon holds great significance, leading to a place where self-doubt fades, self-compassion flourishes, and your inner dialogue becomes your steadfast ally.

Our journey commences with a deep dive into the intricate workings of the human psyche, where negative self-talk often takes root. It's a pervasive presence, subtly undermining our self-esteem, eroding our self-worth, and casting shadows over our potential. As we set out on this adventure, we shall equip ourselves with the insights and the tools required to triumph over our inner challenges.

In Chapter 1, we will explore the origins of negative self-talk, venturing into its hidden depths and uncovering the subtle ways it permeates our daily existence. Through engaging case studies and introspection, we aim to raise your self-awareness, the vital first step toward liberation.

Chapter 2 encourages us to explore the triggers that set off negative self-talk. Together, we'll navigate various life situations where self-doubt tends to emerge – from navigating mistakes to grappling with body image and dealing with performance pressures. By undertaking the exercises and engaging in self-reflection, you'll emerge armed with the strategies necessary to disarm these triggers.

In Chapter 3, we'll venture into the realm of beliefs and self-beliefs, the narratives that have shaped your self-perception. Guided by case studies and introspective prompts, you'll interact with these beliefs with newfound clarity. Transformation commences with rewriting these narratives, shedding the constraints and embracing new and empowering perspectives.

Our final chapter marks a joyous celebration of your inherent worth, your dreams, and your aspirations. We'll challenge, reframe, and de-emphasize negative self-talk, finally dedicating ourselves to self-prioritization. Together, we'll unveil your bucket list, dreams, passions, and aspirations, breathing life into them through visualization, paving the way to a brighter and more positive future.

As you embark on this voyage, always hold in your heart the knowledge that you are priceless and your worth immeasurable. Self-love and empowerment await you at the end of this journey. This book stands as your faithful guide, offering wisdom, strategies, and exercises to illuminate the inner recesses of your being. True transformation commences within you, and it's a journey worth celebrating.

Prepare to conquer negative self-talk, nurture self-compassion, and embrace the most vibrant, empowered version of yourself. The adventure unfolds here and now.

Chapter 1
Identifying Negative-Self Talk

In this chapter, we delve into the nature of negative self-talk, its root causes and how it usually manifests in our lives. We reflect on how your negative self-talk may have developed and why, identifying the patterns of thinking errors which lead to negative self-talk. By means of the practical case studies and exercises, we will explore and practice the skills and tools needed to manage and eventually conquer our negative self-talk.

Before We Start

Take a moment to celebrate your decision to complete this course in the workbook by writing a congratulatory note to yourself. Let yourself feel proud of your commitment and dedication to your personal growth and development.

What is Negative Self-Talk?

Negative self-talk comes from that part of our inner voice that criticizes, judges and demeans us. It's the internal monologue that tells us we're not good enough, that we're failures, that we're unworthy or that makes us doubt ourselves.

Negative self-talk can be subtle and insidious, and often goes unnoticed. Yet it can have a profound impact on our self-esteem, our general well-being, and our unexplored capabilities.

Negative self-talk can take many forms, from blatant criticism to more subtle self-doubt. It can be triggered by various situations, such as facing a challenge, making a mistake, or receiving criticism. It is usually automatic and habitual, and often happens without conscious awareness. It gradually becomes a pervasive and toxic presence in our lives, shaping our beliefs about ourselves and our abilities.

How do you think negative self-talk has affected you in your life?

Negative self-talk can manifest in many thinking errors, including:

- **Overgeneralization:** we draw sweeping conclusions about ourselves based on a single event or situation.
- **Catastrophizing:** we exaggerate the negative consequences of a situation or mistake.
- **Personalization:** we take responsibility for events or situations that are beyond our control.
- **All-or-nothing thinking:** we see things in black-and-white terms, and believe that there is no middle ground.
- **Should statements:** we use "should," "must," or "have to" statements to set unrealistic expectations for ourselves.

Do you engage in any one of the above thinking errors?

What do you typically say to yourself in such circumstances?

Case Studies: Thinking Errors

Over-generalization

Trudy has been trying to lose weight for a few weeks and has been following a strict diet and exercise regimen. One day, she eats a piece of cake at a party and thinks to herself, "I blew my entire diet, I have no self-control." She starts feeling guilty and disappointed in herself, and begins to over-generalize by believing that she will never be able to stick to a healthy diet and will always fail at weight loss.

Kara has also been on a diet and at her mother's birthday party she had some cake which she had promised herself not to have. She acknowledged that she fell off the wagon a little but instead of criticizing herself and engaging in negative self-talk, she also acknowledged that it's okay to indulge in a treat once in a while. She told herself that one piece of cake does not define her entire diet. She reminded herself that it's important to enjoy life and that moderation is key.

Who is more likely to be successful in their weight loss journey?

Write down the reasons why you believe this is so.

Catastrophizing

Jenny, a high school student, is preparing for her final exams. She takes her exams very seriously. She has recently been struggling with calculus and she is becoming worried that she will not do well in the upcoming math test. She begins to catastrophize, thinking that if she fails this one exam, she will fail the entire course, not get into college, and have no future prospects. This leads her to feel overwhelmed and anxious.

Abigail has also been struggling with calculus. She knows that this is not an easy math subject and that many students struggle with it. She tells herself that she knows she's smart because she has had difficult subjects before and still passed the tests. She told herself that it's ok to struggle and to make mistakes. She decided to take action and seek help from her teacher and to focus more on understanding calculus better.

Observe

Jenny is hard on herself in her thinking, whereas Abigail is self-loving and self-compassionate. Jenny makes herself feel worse, whereas Abigail empowers herself by soothing herself and by planning to take action to better her situation.

Reflect

How important, do you think, attitude is, in determining success or failure?

Personalizing

Josh is volunteering at a homeless shelter and notices a man who appears angry and distant. The man refuses to accept Josh's help and Josh takes it personally, believing that he must have done something wrong. He begins to engage in negative self-talk, telling himself that he is not good at helping people and that he should have done better. Josh doesn't consider that the man's behavior may be due to factors outside of his control, such as mental illness or a difficult life circumstance.

In what situations do you sometimes personalize things when in reality they are not in your control?

How could Josh better approach this situation in his own head?

All-or-Nothing

Emma and Rob have been dating for two months. During the weekdays they would video call each other every evening and meet in the weekends. One evening, Rob had to work overtime and couldn't make their usual video call. Emma started to panic and think that their relationship was over. She told herself, "He doesn't love me anymore. I must have done something wrong. I can't live without him. I'll never find someone better." She felt anxious and insecure.

If Emma were to challenge her anxious self-talk and REFRAME it in a more realistic way, how would it sound like?

'Should' and 'Have to' Statements

Melanie had been working tirelessly on a time-share deal with a luxury resort for weeks. She had been putting in extra hours, sacrificing her weekends, and neglecting her personal life to ensure the deal went through. Finally, she received a call from the negotiating partners stating that they had decided to withdraw. Melanie's inner critic immediately kicked in, telling her that she should have done more, worked harder, and that she had to make the deal work. She started blaming herself for the failure of the deal and believed that she had let her company down. She felt like a failure and started to spiral into negative self-talk, convinced that her career was over.

Observe & Reflect

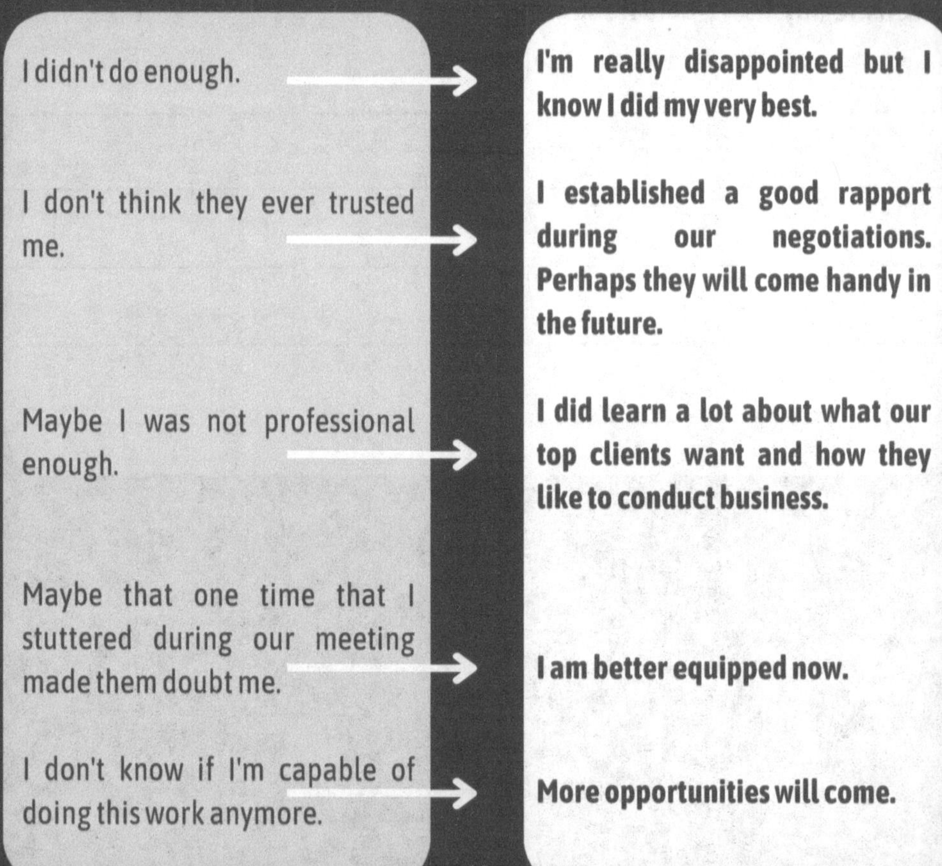

Empowered

What positive aspects can I identify in this situation or in myself, to make me feel empowered?

Motivated

I embrace setbacks as opportunities for growth.

Resilient

How can I practice self-compassion and focus on progress, to overcome challenges?

Cut and display prominently, to remind yourself daily.

Where does Negative Self-Talk come from?

Negative self-talk comes from **consistent training of the brain,** stemming from the negative experiences that we have lived since our earliest years. They accumulate over time by being repeatedly retained and anticipated by the brain. This cycle perpetuates negative thoughts and beliefs giving rise to our negative self-talk. It becomes an unconscious and habitual pattern of thought. Many times we do not realize that we are engaged in negative self-thought. Additionally, we may have become accustomed to filtering out the positive aspects of a situation, focusing solely on the negative. As a result, we repeatedly reinforce certain negative and limiting beliefs about ourselves and our abilities without realizing it.

Our negative self-talk is a by-product of this consistent brain training. It is not entirely our fault that we have been caught up in this negative thought cycle because our brain has made deductions, based on its interpretation of experiences.

Negative self-talk may be tied to strong emotions such as fear, shame and guilt. When we experience these emotions we fall in the trap of demeaning ourselves in our minds, doubting our abilities and our self-worth. For example, if we feel shame about something that we did, we start thinking that we are are worthless. Similarly, if we feel guilty about something, we start to think that we are a bad person and don't deserve good things in life.

Fear, shame and guilt erode our self-worth.

By embracing self-acceptance and cultivating self-compassion, we liberate ourselves from being defined and controlled by these powerful emotions.

Acknowledge these emotions but do not allow them to define you.

Overcoming Negative Self-Talk: the basic tools.

Negative self-talk tends to happen automatically and mechanically. By consciously shedding light on our repeated thought patterns and beliefs, we can begin to recognize them more clearly and take the necessary steps to overcome them.

The primary basic tools which will assist us in eradicating negative self-talk are:

(i) conscious awareness of our negative self-talk;

(ii) placing distance between ourselves and negative self-talk;

(ii) attention to positive and empowering thoughts.

These tools provide valuable insights into your negative self-talk. They act as a beacon, illuminating the patterns and frequency of self-criticism that often remain concealed. Think of your negative self-talk as hidden objects waiting to be discovered through conscious awareness—the light that exposes them. Many times, we're oblivious to most of our negative self-talk until we shine this light upon them, making them discoverable and empowering us to take action.

As you practice conscious awareness of your negative self-talk, a notable shift will occur. You'll naturally create some distance between yourself and these self-critical thoughts. This newfound perspective grants you the ability to scrutinize these negative statements, questioning their validity and accuracy.

This initial step paves the way for a transformative habit: **the ability to intercept and halt the progression of negative self-talk in its tracks.** This skill is the foundation for a subsequent empowering habit: **allocating more mental real estate to positive thoughts while diminishing the significance of negative chatter.**

Conscious Awareness of Negative Self-Talk

It is impossible to change something that you are not aware of. To begin the journey of dissolving negative self-talk, it is crucial that you start paying close attention to your thoughts and the language within your inner dialogue. At first, this might feel overwhelming as you actively listen to your mind's chatter, but this is entirely normal as you work to develop conscious awareness of your thought patterns.

Awareness is the foundation of change. It is the catalyst for transformation. If we're unaware of our negative self-talk when it occurs, we can't effectively challenge or replace it with more positive thoughts. Nor can we develop strategies to eliminate it. Negative self-talk can become deeply ingrained due to repeated mental conditioning. However, practicing awareness helps reverse this process. When we become conscious of our negative self-talk, we can start observing it from a more objective perspective, allowing us to challenge its validity.

Practicing awareness marks the initial stage of your journey to conquer your negative self-talk. Throughout this process, be patient with yourself, in the knowledge that you are taking the right steps to dismantle your negative self-talk habit. As you continue to practice, you'll find it becomes more manageable over time.

In the upcoming section, you will begin cultivating awareness through a structured practice. A table has been provided to assist you in tracking both the frequency of your negative self-talk and your growing awareness of it.

- **Pay attention by being in the moment and focusing SOLELY on what you are doing.**

- **On recognizing a negative statement about yourself, STOP. Recognize that your mind is chattering negatively. Don't indulge in it. Let it go.**

- **Distract yourself from the thought by doing something physical** (clear a table, wash your coffee cup, get up and move around),

OR

- **Force yourself to think of one thing that you like about yourself and say it to yourself** (this could be appreciation for a bodily or facial feature, a part of your personality, or a recent thing you've done which makes you proud or happy).

Reflect

When you start creating distance between yourself and your negative self-talk, you will soon realize that your thoughts are not always accurate, and your emotions do not necessarily reflect reality.

Here is a table for you to fill in when practicing awareness. You will only need to fill this in at the beginning. With time, you will instantly become aware of your negative self-talk and apply the steps.

My Negative Self-Talk	I became Instantly Aware	I didn't become Instantly Aware	I was able to Stop	I was unable to Stop

My Negative Self-Talk	I became Instantly Aware	I didn't become Instantly Aware	I was able to Stop	I was unable to Stop

Identifying Situations of Your Negative Self-Talk.

Take a moment to recognize the situations that tend to trigger your negative self-talk. Choose the situations that you feel apply to you.

Write down the situation AND your negative self-talk statement which usually accompanies it. Jot down your answers in the next page.

This exercise will help you gain awareness and develop a deeper understanding of your thought patterns.

1. I tend to feel anxious and stressed when

2. I compare myself to others and feel bad when

3. I felt like a failure and not good enough when

4. I tend to second-guess myself when

5. I feel overwhelmed and unable to handle things when

6. I felt rejected and excluded when

7. I felt judged and criticized when

8. I felt that I didn't fit in or belong when

1

2

3

4

5

6

7

8

1. I feel that I am not valued and appreciated when

2. I feel that I am not living up to my expectations when

3. I feel that I am not being true to myself and my values when

4. I feel insecure or self-conscious when

5. I feel that I'm not being heard or understood when

6. I feel that I'm not doing enough when

1

2

3

4

5

6

Practice Placing Distance from Your Negative Self-Talk

Talking to Your Best Friend

Hannah: Emily, I messed up at work today. I made a mistake in the accounts, and then I tried to cover it up so that no one would find out. But now I'm so worried. What if they discover it in the next audit? I keep replaying everything in my mind and it feels like I'm going crazy.

Emily: Hannah, take a deep breath and tell me more about the mistake. Is there any way you can remedy it or address it directly with your boss?

Hannah: I can't believe I made such a huge mistake. I'm so incompetent. How could I be so careless? Now I've covered it up, and I'm just waiting for everything to come crashing down. I'm going to lose my job, and everyone will see what a failure I am.

Emily: Hannah, you're feeling overwhelmed right now. Try not to be too hard on yourself. Mistakes happen, and it's not a reflection of your worth as a person. You're doing the best you can. I want you to think of all the other jobs that you did so well. Remember when you managed to get a tax rebate for the company and how pleased your boss was?

Hannah: Yes, he was so pleased. I felt so accomplished that day.

Emily: We all make mistakes Hannah. Give yourself some time and stop dwelling over it. I'm sure that with a fresh head, you'll find the solution. I don't think that your boss is going to look at this one mistake and not take into account how well you perform overall.

Hannah: Yes, I genuinely love my job and I always do my best. I'll sleep over it and decide what to do tomorrow.

Emily: Great! I'm more than positive that you will find a solution. And who knows, this could be a blessing in disguise for you.

Hannah: Thank you Emily, for always being there for me.

An effective method to practice placing distance between yourself and your negative self-talk is to imagine your best friend pouring out her worries to you, and criticizing herself. Can you answer the following questions about the conversation between Hannah and Emily?

What emotional state was Hannah in?

What did Emily do to avert Hannah from spiralling into self-criticizm?

How did Hannah make herself feel better?

How can Hannah benefit from shifting to self-compassion in this situation?

Suggested answers are provided in the next page.

What emotional state was Hannah in?

She was feeling anxious and scared. She was catastrophizing the situation, focusing on her mistake and anticipating the worst consequence.

What did Emily do to avert Hannah from spiralling into self-criticizm?

She reminded Hannah of past accomplishments in order to bring balance to Hannah's thinking.

How did Hannah make herself feel better?

She allowed herself to think about a time when she had performed her job well and was appreciated for her success.

How can Hannah benefit from shifting to self-compassion in this situation?

She places some distance between herself and her negative self-talk. This will allow her to clear her mind and look at the situation with less emotions and more objectivity.

Ashley is feeling overwhelmed and defeated. Her boyfriend is very close to his mother and she cannot handle his mother's constant intrusion in their lives. She is venting with you about her feelings.

"I just can't handle his mother's constant intrusion in our lives. She's always crossing boundaries and acting like she knows what's best for us. I feel suffocated."

Ashley continues to vent, her negative self-talk beginning to take hold. "I'm just not good enough for him or his family. I can't compete with his mother's influence, and I fear it's going to drive us apart. "

What would you tell your best friend in this situation?

Suggested reflections are provided in the next page.

It's challenging when there are differences and conflicts within a relationship, especially when it involves parents. But remember, you are an amazing person with your own worth. You don't have to compete or change who you are to fit into their expectations. Perhaps it's time to have an open and honest conversation with your boyfriend about your feelings. Share your concerns and discuss potential boundaries that could be set with his parents. Remember, communication is key in any relationship, and finding a compromise that works for both of you is crucial.

Amanda's colleague asked her for a favor. She accepted because she didn't want her friend to think that she was selfish or unsympathetic. After all, her colleague had helped her many times in the past.

Later that day Amanda started having an uncomfortable feeling. Deep down she didn't want to do what her friend had asked her. She vents her frustration with you.

"I can't believe I said yes again. I knew deep down that I didn't want to do it, but I couldn't bring myself to say no. I always end up feeling so weak and taken advantage of. I should have been stronger. I shouldn't have let myself get into this situation in the first place. I'm such a pushover."

What would you tell your best friend in this situation?

Suggested reflections are provided in the next page.

We all have moments when we struggle to assert ourselves. It doesn't mean that you're weak. It means you're compassionate and kind-hearted. But it's important to find a balance between being helpful and taking care of yourself. It starts with practicing self-compassion and setting clear boundaries. When someone asks for a favor, take a moment to check in with yourself. Ask yourself if it aligns with your values and if you have the capacity to take it on. Remember, saying no doesn't make you a bad person. It means you're being true to yourself.

Giving attention to anything entails a decision that you make. You hold the power to decide what you are willing to give your attention to and not. When you give attention to negative self-talk you are empowering and reinforcing it, validating underlying negative beliefs that you have about yourself. **Make a conscious decision that from now onwards you are NOT going to give your attention to your negative self-talk.**

Having awareness of your negative self-talk is important to conquer it. However, this is where you stop. You don't keep dwelling on it or repeating it in your head. Instead, you start to practice detachment from it. The more you practice, the weaker its grip on you will become. This practice will pave the way to taking action in Chapter 4 where we will have practiced enough distance from our negative self-talk to be able to challenge, reframe and de-emphasize it effectively.

In the next exercise you will decide where you habitually place your attention by choosing the answer that best reflects your reaction to challenging situations.

When faced with a challenging task, do you habitually:

1. think about the potential obstacles — **NEGATIVE**
2. focus on the potential opportunities — **POSITIVE**

When you make a mistake, do you habitually:

1. dwell on the error — **NEGATIVE**
2. criticize yourself — **NEGATIVE**
3. ignore it — **POSITIVE**
4. view it as a lesson — **POSITIVE**

When receiving feedback or criticism, do you:

1. become defensive — **NEGATIVE**
2. dwell on the criticism — **NEGATIVE**
3. extract constructive insights — **POSITIVE**

When you are rejected by someone, do you:

1. see it as a reflection of your worth — **NEGATIVE**
2. accept it as a part of life — **POSITIVE**

When you are stressed, do you:

1. soothe yourself — **POSITIVE**
2. criticize yourself — **NEGATIVE**
3. stop and take a break — **POSITIVE**
4. dwell on the stressful situation — **NEGATIVE**

When facing a setback, do you:

1. doubt your abilities — **NEGATIVE**
2. decide that it's impossible — **NEGATIVE**
3. remind yourself of your end goal — **POSITIVE**
4. feel more determined to succeed. — **POSITIVE**

Positive Focus Benefits

1. **Improved Mental Health:** Positive thinking can reduce symptoms of anxiety and depression. It helps in managing stress better, leading to improved overall mental well-being.
2. **Enhanced Resilience:** Positive thinkers tend to bounce back more effectively from setbacks and challenges. They see these situations as opportunities for growth and learning.
3. **Better Physical Health:** Optimistic individuals often experience better physical health outcomes. They are more likely to engage in healthy behaviors, like regular exercise and a balanced diet.
4. **Increased Productivity:** Positive thinking can enhance focus and motivation. It helps people stay on track with their goals and complete tasks efficiently.
5. **Enhanced Relationships:** Positive individuals tend to have healthier and more fulfilling relationships. Their optimism and supportive attitudes can lead to stronger social connections and improved communication.

Now that you've initiated the active practice of conscious awareness concerning your negative self-talk and where your habitual focus lies in various situations, it's the opportune moment to introduce two foundational principles. These values will be pivotal throughout the rest of your journey.

(i) Practicing Self-love and Self-compassion

(ii) Prioritizing your thoughts by challenging, reframing and de-emphasizing your negative self-talk

(iii) Practicing the previous two points consistently .

When we practice self-love and self-compassion, we become more aware of our needs and treat ourselves with the same care and compassion we would show to a dear friend.

Learning to be kind to yourself takes practice. Start by offering kind and supportive words to yourself, to replace your harsh criticism and judgment. Make yourself one of your top priorities like you would with your own children, your partner or your parents. Allow some time to take care of yourself physically. Eat good and healthy food. Get enough sleep and relaxation time. Say no when you don't feel up to something or someone. Place yourself first as much as you possibly can. Practice being in the moment and not in your head. Focus on what is happening now. Forgive yourself always because everybody makes mistakes. Feel grateful for all that you have in your life and all that surrounds you. Find the positive in every single situation or person in your life.

The upcoming exercises will systematically guide you toward a deeper sense of self-acceptance and self-worth. They will encourage you to heighten your awareness of the levels of self-love and self-compassion you extend to yourself and pinpoint areas where you need to nurture these qualities more.

Practicing Self-Love and Self-Compassion

Take a look at the list below. Each one is connected to self-love and self-compassion. In what areas of your life do you need to be kinder and more loving to yourself? Choose the ones that are more applicable to you, reflect on its definition and how you can practice this quality more in your life.

Self-acknowledgment

Self-acknowledgment is the act of recognizing and accepting yourself, including your thoughts, feelings, strengths, and weaknesses, without judgment.

Where do I need to acknowledge myself?

Self-Appreciation

Self-appreciation is recognizing and valuing your personal qualities, accomplishments, and worth.

Where do I need to appreciate myself more?

Self-Respect

Self-respect is valuing and protecting your own personal limits, values, and needs, maintaining healthy boundaries and prioritizing your well-being.

Where do I need to respect myself more?

Self-Worth

Self-worth is to recognize your inherent worthiness, irrespective of external validation or comparison to others.

Where do I need to acknowledge my worth irrespective of external validation?

Self-Acceptance

Self-acceptance is embracing yourself fully, including flaws and past mistakes and letting go of shame or guilt in the knowledge that you've grown from past mistakes.

Where do I need to accept myself and let go of my guilt or shame?

Self-Care

Self-care is the ability to take action to nurture your physical, mental and emotional needs. It is to intentionally prioritize nurturing activities such as getting enough sleep, eating nourishing foods, engaging in regular exercise, practicing stress management techniques, setting boundaries, seeking support when needed, engaging in activities that bring joy and relaxation, and cultivating self-compassion and self-reflection.

What needs am I neglecting?

Self-Trust

Self-Trust is your inner reliance and faith in yourself to make choices that align with your personal values and goals. It involves listening to your intuition, being honest with yourself, and having the courage to take risks and learn from mistakes.

Where do I need to doubt myself less?

Self-Kindness

Self-kindness is treating yourself with gentleness, compassion, and understanding. It involves extending the same care and kindness that one would offer to a dear friend or loved one.

Where do I need to be kinder to myself?

Self-Forgiveness

Self-forgiveness is acknowledging past mistakes and the lessons learned while releasing the burden of self-judgment, guilt or shame.

Where do I need to forgive myself and let go of my guilt or shame?

End of Chapter Reflection

Take a moment to reflect on what you've learned so far:

1. Awareness: Have you gained a greater awareness of when and where your negative self-talk tends to occur in your life? Are there specific situations or triggers that stand out?

2. Patterns: Have you identified any recurring patterns or common themes in your negative self-talk? Are there particular thinking errors you've recognized?

____

____

____

3. Impact: What insights have you gained into how negative self-talk affects your daily life, emotions, and self-esteem? Have you noticed any specific areas where it has a significant impact?

____

____

____

4. Resolutions: As you've delved into these questions, have you made any resolutions or commitments for change? Are there specific strategies or tools from this chapter that you plan to apply in your daily life?

____

____

____

Chapter 2
The Triggers of Negative Self-Talk

In this chapter we'll explore the nuances of negative self-talk, including the different forms it can take and the situations that trigger it. Here are some situations which commonly trigger negative self-talk:

1. Making mistakes
2. Social Situations
3. Challenges and Setbacks
4. Comparing ourselves to Others
5. Body Image
6. Performance Pressure

We will delve into each of the situations mentioned above in your life through a series of reflective exercises. The questions within each exercise are structured to guide you towards forming well-informed conclusions about the triggers of your negative self-talk. This will pave the way to taking action in Chapter 4, where you will be ready to commit to practicing and taking appropriate action to conquer your negative self-talk.

Making Mistakes

Making mistakes is a common trigger for negative self-talk. When we make a mistake, we beat ourselves up for it and tell ourselves that we're not good enough or that we'll never get it right.

Think of a mistake that you have done in the past and that has caused you to feel like a failure. Then answer the questions.

What thoughts immediately came to mind after making the mistake?

Did you dwell on the mistake and replayed it in your mind?

How did you criticize yourself? What words did you use?

Did you make generalizations about yourself based on one mistake?

How did your self-talk affect your emotions and behavior after making the mistake?

Judge your Answers: my informed conclusions

Reflect on the answers that you have just written as if it was not you who had written them. From the answers given, you are going to identify and write down your observations about the following factors:

Frequency: do you notice that you engage in negative self-talk after every mistake or does this happen only when you judge the mistake to be a big one?

If this happens every time you make a mistake, irrespective of how big or small it is, this may indicate that there is a pattern and a habit. If your negative self-talk is triggered only when you judge the mistake to be very big, the pattern in you is not as entrenched. This will tell you the degree of awareness that you will have to practice in order to dissolve this pattern.

Intensity: can you decide on how intense your negative self-talk was? Was it very harsh, critical and demotivating?

Accuracy: can you identify whether your negative self-talk was based on absolutely true facts or were there assumptions that you made that may not have been completely true?

How can you become more compassionate with yourself when you make a mistake or feel that you did not do something well enough? Reflect on how you can be kinder to yourself in your self-talk and write down the statements you could use.

Social Situations

Social situations can trigger our negative self-talk when we don't meet our own expectations in how we present ourselves. We often strive to showcase the best version of ourselves, but when we fall short, we tend to engage in self-criticism. This self-critique may also arise when we feel that we're being judged or evaluated by others. Such situations can activate a range of negative emotions, including fear of rejection, self-consciousness, perfectionism, negative self-image, comparison to others, fear of embarrassment, and general social anxiety.

The upcoming exercise will provide you with insights into your negative self-talk triggers and patterns in social situations.

What are the worries that you tend to have when attending social situations?

____

____

____

____

____

____

____

How do you typically feel before entering a social situation? Anxious, excited, relaxed or something else? Why, do you think, do you feel this way?

____

____

____

____

What specific negative thoughts run through your mind when you're in social settings? Try to recall some recent situations and the thoughts associated with them.

____

____

____

____

How do you typically behave in social settings?

____

____

Are there particular triggers or patterns in social situations that tend to activate your negative self-talk? (e.g. meeting new people, speaking in public, social gatherings).

____

____

____

____

Have you noticed any recurring themes in your negative self-talk during social interactions? (e.g. self-doubt, fear of judment).

____

____

____

____

____

____

What type of social gathering are you usually very comfortable in? (e.g. people you know, family, friends). Why is this so?

Reflect on how this is different from the social situations where you tend to feel uncomfortable and anxious. What difference stands out between these two scenarios?

Practicing Positive Affirmations and Constructive Thought for Social Situations

We've all experienced it: negative self-talk that arises during social events, triggered by conversations, thoughts about others or ourselves, or even the environment around us. In such moments, we often find ourselves unprepared because we haven't yet trained our minds sufficiently in constructive thinking and positive affirmations.

Practicing positive affirmations and cultivating constructive thoughts is an ongoing effort. It equips us to approach life's events with confidence and inner calm.

Here are some constructive thoughts and positive affirmations you can practice before attending social events. The following inner dialogue can be a transformative tool in how you feel when participating in social gatherings:

When I catch myself engaging in negative self-talk in social situations, I can replace it with positive affirmations and constructive thoughts. For example, if I start thinking, 'Everyone here is judging me,' I can remind myself that people are often more focused on their own insecurities. So, I could affirm, **'I am just as worthy as anyone else here, and I have something valuable to offer.'**

If I feel self-conscious about my appearance or what I'm saying, I can replace those thoughts with, **'I am unique, and that's something worth celebrating,'** *or* **'I'm here to connect, and it's okay to be imperfect.'** *Moreover, instead of assuming people won't like me, I can remind myself,* **'I possess great qualities and interests that some people will appreciate, and those are the connections I'm seeking.'**

By consciously substituting negative self-talk with these affirmations and constructive thoughts, I can begin to shift my mindset and feel more confident and at ease in social situations.

Challenges and Setbacks

Challenges and setbacks can seem overwhelming when we're in the midst of them. Yet, as time passes and we gain perspective, our perception of the challenge often shifts. It may appear less daunting or significant than our initial experience.

There are several reasons for this shift in perception. Firstly, our emotions can influence how we perceive a situation, amplifying its intensity. When faced with a challenge, strong emotions like fear, anxiety, or frustration may distort our perception, making the situation appear more formidable than it is when viewed objectively.

Furthermore, our brains naturally prioritize immediate threats and challenges over long-term concerns. When confronted with a challenge, our brains may perceive it as more urgent than it truly is. With time, as we distance ourselves from the situation, our brains gain the perspective to realize it wasn't as urgent as initially believed.

Finally, when we reflect on a challenge after it has passed, we often benefit from hindsight. This perspective allows us to see how the situation unfolded and realize that it might not have been as daunting as we initially perceived it. Moreover, we may identify ways in which we've grown or learned from the experience, leading to a shift in our perception of the challenge from something negative to something positive and transformative.

One significant challenge we all encounter at some point in life is the loss of a loved one. This emotionally charged situation can be overwhelming, with the feeling that the loss is insurmountable and recovery seems distant.

As time passes, our perception of the loss evolves. While sadness and grief remain, we begin to view the situation differently. We may recognize personal growth or lessons learned, and we often shift our focus to the positive memories shared with our loved one.

This shift often results from the passage of time and the process of grief and mourning, which allow us to heal and process our emotions. Understanding that our perception of loss can change with time grants us the freedom to grieve and heal at our own pace.

The following exercise will provide insight into your past and present perceptions of challenges and setbacks in your life. This is followed by a specific exercise dealing with the loss of a loved one.

Can you describe a challenge or setback that you faced in your life, and the thoughts and feelings that arose in response?

On looking back, can you describe how it makes you feel now?

____

____

Does it still have the effect it had at the time? Why do you think so?

____

____

Can you describe how you coped with this challenge/setback at the time?

____

____

____

Can you describe how you would cope with it differently now?

____

____

____

____

____

Can you find one positive element in this whole situation? *(This question may feel artificial but I do urge you to think of at least one positive aspect or result that emerged from this challenge or setback.)*

____

____

____

Can you identify what you have learned from this experience and how this has transformed you?

____

____

____

____

Do you feel that you are better equipped now than you were before? Why?

____

____

____

____

The Loss of a Loved One

Dealing with the loss of a loved one is an immensely challenging and deeply emotional experience. It's a profound and inevitable part of the human condition, a journey that most of us will undertake at some point in our lives. In the aftermath of such a loss, the world can appear darker, and the burden of grief can be overwhelming. However, within that darkness, there lies the potential for personal growth, healing, and the discovery of inner strength.

Allow yourself the space to grieve; it's a unique journey for each person, with no prescribed right or wrong way to experience it. Embrace the feelings of sadness, anger, and confusion as they come. Seek support from those close to you, individuals you trust completely, as their emotional support can be an invaluable asset during the grieving process. In your pursuit of self-care, take small but significant steps, like going for a short walk, indulging in long, soothing showers, and prioritizing rest.

Discover meaningful ways to celebrate the life of your loved one. Gradually shift your focus from the void of loss to the positive memories you shared with them. Remembering and cherishing your loved one is a beautiful way to maintain a lasting connection.

In the following exercises, we will delve deeper into the profound challenges that accompany the loss of someone dear and offer a more positive way to navigate this profoundly emotional journey. While the pain may never completely dissipate, there are paths to finding solace and honoring the enduring memories of those we have lost.

What are some cherished memories you shared with your loved one?

____

____

____

____

Have you thought about creating a memory book or tribute in honor of your loved one? If yes, make a plan for the memory book.

____

____

____

____

____

How can you incorporate your loved one's values into your life moving forward?

____

____

____

____

What acts of kindness or service can you engage in to honor your loved one's memory?

____

____

____

____

____

Can you think of a creative outlet or hobby that you can pursue as a form of self-expression and healing?

____

____

____

____

____

What small steps can you take to prioritize self-care in your daily routine?

____

____

____

____

____

Monday	Tuesday
Wednesday	Thursday
Friday	Saturday
Sunday	TOP PRIORITIES

Week 1	Week 2
Week 3	Week 4
Week 5	Week 6
Week 7	**TOP PRIORITIES**

Comparing Ourselves to Others

Comparing ourselves to others can trigger negative self-talk when we perceive that we fall short in some way, whether in terms of our achievements, appearance, or abilities. This can lead to feelings of insecurity, self-doubt, and low self-esteem, which, in turn, can fuel negative self-talk.

Underlying negative beliefs that contribute to negative self-talk when comparing ourselves to others include feelings of inadequacy, perfectionism, self-doubt, negative self-image, and unrealistic expectations. For instance, believing that one is not good enough compared to others can fuel negative self-talk and feelings of inferiority. Thinking that one must be perfect in every way can lead to negative self-talk when perceiving that they have fallen short of this ideal. Similarly, the belief that one is not capable or competent enough can fuel negative self-talk when making comparisons to others who appear to be more successful or accomplished.

In the next exercise, you will reflect on the comparisons you make in your life and their impact on your self-esteem.

In what ways do you compare yourself to others? List the situations in which you find yourself making these comparisons.

____

____

____

____

What do you tell yourself in these situations?

____

____

List the reasons that lead you to believe you don't measure up to the standards of the people you compare yourself to.

____

____

____

Do you ever compare your intelligence to others? What do you tell yourself in these situations? What do you believe to be true, that makes you feel that you are not as intelligent?

____

____

____

____

____

____

How does comparing your capabilities to others trigger your negative self-talk? Can you list the capabilities which you think are missing in yourself?

____

____

____

____

____

When comparing your career or professional success to others, how do you feel? Write down the thoughts that you usually have.

____

____

____

____

____

____

If you are in a romantic or long-term relationship, what comparisons do you make in relation to other couples? Does this trigger negative self-talk? If yes, can you write down what you would like to experience more of and what you would not like to experience anymore?

Do you compare your family or upbringing to that of others? What feelings do you have when you think about your childhood? Are there things which you would have liked not to experience in your childhood? How does this make you feel right now?

How do you react when your best friend achieves success or accomplishments? Describe your feelings.

____

____

____

____

How do you react when someone you know achieves success or accomplishments which you desire? Describe how this makes you feel.

____

____

____

____

Judge your Answers: my informed conclusions

Review the responses you have written and consider the following questions to gain deeper insights into your self-esteem.

How would you define self-esteem?

____

____

On looking back at your answers, what do they say about your self-esteem. (*Look at the answers as if you are reading someone else's reflections.*) **Are you any one of the following?**

(i) I am a perfectionist. Nothing that I do or am is perfect enough for me.

(ii) I doubt myself often. I am not sure about my capabilities.

(iii) I feel like I am a victim of others. My life circumstances have not been fair to me.

(iv) I have feelings of resentfulness because there are goals that I have not achieved.

(v) Other _______________________________________

____

Body Image

Negative self-talk related to body image often originates from societal standards, comparisons to others, past experiences of bullying or body shaming, and personal insecurities. Unrealistic ideals of perfection can lead us to perceive our bodies as objects open to external evaluation, triggering self-deprecating thoughts. Moreover, shame, often rooted in previous negative experiences or messages, contributes to self-perceived flaws.

Shame and guilt concerning body image extend beyond mere negative self-talk, profoundly affecting our overall well-being. Feelings of shame can erode our self-worth, distorting our self-perception and impacting various aspects of life, from self-esteem and relationships to work and overall quality of life. It can also isolate us as we hide perceived flaws and withdraw from social situations.

Societal pressures and unrealistic beauty standards often fuel shame and guilt, perpetuating a harmful cycle of self-punishment and the pursuit of unattainable ideals. In addition to fostering negative self-talk, guilt can drive detrimental behaviors like extreme dieting, excessive exercise, or risky cosmetic procedures, all in an attempt to conform to these external standards. These behaviors not only jeopardize physical health but also maintain feelings of inadequacy and dissatisfaction. Ultimately, the harmful repercussions of shame and guilt on body image extend far beyond our inner dialogue, influencing our actions, relationships, and overall psychological well-being.

Remember, while this exploration may uncover the detrimental impact of shame and guilt, it also sheds light on the potential for change and healing, emphasizing the importance of self-acceptance and self-compassion in our journey towards a healthier body image.

Embracing My Body

Embracing and loving our bodies as they are is a powerful act of self-compassion and self-love. Our bodies are unique, carrying with them the stories of our lives and the experiences that have shaped us. Instead of fixating on societal ideals or unrealistic standards, we can choose to honor and appreciate our bodies for their resilience and the incredible work they do every day. True self-acceptance begins when we look in the mirror and say, 'I am enough just as I am.' **It's about celebrating our bodies not despite their imperfections but because of them.** When we cultivate self-love and body positivity, we foster a deeper connection with ourselves and experience a profound sense of freedom and confidence.

When you look at yourself in the mirror, what are the first thoughts or words that come to your mind regarding your body's appearance?

Have you ever avoided certain social situations or activities because you felt self-conscious about your body? If so, can you recall the thoughts that fueled this avoidance?

Think about a time when you received a compliment about your appearance. Did you genuinely accept it, or did negative self-talk prevent you from fully embracing the compliment?

____

____

____

____

Reflect on moments when you've felt a strong desire to change your body in some way, such as through diets, intense workouts, or cosmetic procedures. What thoughts and beliefs were driving these desires, and how did they make you feel about yourself?

____

____

____

____

____

____

____

Judge your Answers: my informed conclusions

Look back at your responses. What can you conclude about the way you perceive your body?

1. My body image is extremely important for my self-esteem.
2. My body image is important but what's on the inside is way more important.
3. I don't believe I have an attractive body.
4. I believe that I can improve my body appearance and feel good about it.
5. I don't believe that I can improve my body appearance.
6. My negative self-talk about my body is worse than how my body actually looks like.

Other ____

____

My Reflections and Insights:

____

____

____

____

Performance Pressure

Performance pressure, whether it's related to work, sports, or a hobby, can trigger negative self-talk. This occurs when we feel that our performance is being evaluated or judged. Negative self-talk can tell us that we're not good enough or that we'll fail, and it's often based on negative beliefs about our abilities. These beliefs may include the expectation of perfection, self-doubt, and a fear of failure. Additionally, negative self-concepts in the area of performance can arise from comparing ourselves to others or from past negative experiences.

Think of a situation in your life where you felt under pressure that you had to perform very well. Describe how it made you feel.

____

____

____

____

Write down the negative chatter that you told yourself.

____

____

____

____

____

Judge your Answers: my informed conclusions

On looking back at this situation, decide how the negative thoughts and the negative self-chatter escalated your negative experience of the situation.

Do you believe that the negative self-talk affected the outcome of your performance? Explain why, in detail.

____

____

____

____

____

Had you performed in the absence of any negative self-talk, how would you have felt?

____

____

____

____

Criticism and Rejection

When faced with criticism or rejection, it is common to internalize these negative experiences by ruminating over them. This may involve engaging in negative self-talk that perpetuates feelings of self-blame and self-doubt. We may believe that there is something inherently wrong with us and that we are not good enough.

Distinguishing between two forms of criticism is essential: those expressed in frustration or anger, and those expressed with care and respect. Regardless of the type, we tend to internalize criticism and engage in negative self-talk that includes self-blame and self-doubt. Even when criticism is offered with good intentions, our negative self-chatter persists. Dealing with constructive criticism in our head involves recognizing that criticism, even when well-intentioned, can trigger negative self-talk. **The first step is to separate the criticism from our own self-worth and to view it objectively as an opportunity for growth and improvement.** This means taking a step back from our emotions and evaluating the criticism based on its validity and potential for positive change. When faced with non-constructive criticism, a conflict with the critic can trigger opposing reactions in our negative self-talk. We may either internalize their criticism, leading to a spiral of negative self-talk, or dismiss it due to the existing animosity. In both scenarios, it's crucial for personal growth to assess the criticism's validity. Can any of it be utilized for self-improvement? Additionally, consider reflecting on any positive aspects of the situation that the critic may have missed.

Rejection, whether occurring within personal relationships or in our careers, can wield a profound impact on our lives, particularly when we ruminate on it excessively. We understand that rejection is a universal experience but when it is directed at us, our negative self-talk can intensify. Recognizing this trigger is crucial, as it can lead to a particularly destructive form of negative self-talk known as 'confirmation bias.' When we succumb to confirmation bias, we permit our core negative beliefs about ourselves to resurface, actively seeking out evidence that validates these pessimistic beliefs. It is imperative to pause and redirect our thoughts when we become aware of this.

How would you define criticism?

____

____

How would you define rejection?

____

____

When someone criticizes or disagrees with you, how do you typically react? Do you take it to heart or dismiss it easily?

____

____

Think of a situation in your life when you felt rejected. How did you feel at the time? Write down the negative talk that you told yourself.

____

____

____

Think of a situation where you criticized someone. Why did you criticize them?

____

____

What were the thoughts that you had which supported the criticism that you offered?

____

____

____

Was the criticism that you offered connected to an idea that you had about the worthiness of that person? If not, what was it about?

____

____

Think of a situation in your life when you rejected someone. What were your reasons for rejecting them?

____

____

Describe the feelings and thoughts you had about rejecting them.

____

Judge your Answers: my informed conclusions

Look back at the two situations, the one in which you were criticized or rejected and the other in which you yourself criticized or rejected someone. How did your self-talk differ in these two situations?

After having reflected on these two situations, has your perception of criticism and rejection changed? If yes, how would you define criticism and rejection now? If no, would you say that when you criticized or rejected that person, you were doing so based on the worth of that person?

Chapter 3
Beliefs

Human beliefs are complex and multifaceted, shaped by a variety of factors that include cognitive processes, personal experiences, social influences, and cultural background. Our beliefs are influenced by the way we process and interpret information, including our attention, memory, and reasoning abilities. People tend to remember information that confirms their existing beliefs and discount information that contradicts them. Our personal experiences also play a significant role in molding our beliefs. Positive and negative events that happen to us throughout our lives can create cognitive biases that affect the way we interpret new information.

Factors Influencing our Beliefs

Childhood experiences play a very significant role in shaping our self-talk and beliefs about ourselves. Our experiences with our parents, caregivers and other significant individuals shape our attitudes towards ourselves and others, and influence the development of positive or negative self-talk.

One of the ways in which childhood experiences influence our self-talk is through parental modeling. Children learn from their parents and other caregivers, including their attitudes towards themselves and others. If parents are overly critical, children learn to do the same to themselves, leading to negative beliefs about themselves and their abilities. Conversely, childhood experiences of support and encouragement leads to positive beliefs and positive self-talk.

The attachment style developed throughout childhood with primary caregivers has a profound impact on our self-talk and beliefs about ourselves. A child raised with a secure attachment style, with positive and supportive caregivers, is more likely to have positive self-talk and high self-esteem. On the other hand, a child who experienced neglect, abuse, or other forms of maltreatment from their caregivers is more likely to develop negative self-talk and low self-esteem.

Our childhood experiences also influence our perceptions and interpretation of information. Negative experiences during childhood can lead to negative perceptions, where the child often interprets information through the lens of doubt, fear, or a sense of unworthiness. These negative perceptions persist into adulthood and contribute to negative self-talk patterns. The same is true for positive experiences where the child feels loved and safe. This child is likely to be more open-minded, curious, and receptive to new ideas and experiences. They may approach new information with a sense of wonder and excitement, rather than skepticism or fear. Such a child may be more willing to explore different perspectives and viewpoints, rather than rejecting them outright. They may also be more likely to ask questions and seek out further information, rather than making assumptions or drawing conclusions based on limited information. Moreover, a child who feels safe and loved is more likely to have a sense of self-worth and confidence which influences the way in which they interpret information.

Our beliefs and patterns of self-talk are also shaped by our social environment and emotions. The people around us, including family, friends, peers, and authority figures, shape our social environment and influence the beliefs we hold about ourselves. We tend to adopt the beliefs of those we hold in high regard and conform to social norms. In addition, emotions such as our fears, desires, and hopes can also influence our beliefs and patterns of self-talk. We are more likely to adopt beliefs that align with our emotions or help us feel safe or secure.

It is essential to recognize the impact of our beliefs and patterns of self-talk on our behavior, emotions, and well-being. Therefore, it is crucial to critically evaluate and reflect on them to ensure they align with our values, goals, and aspirations. We can use critical thinking, self-reflection, and open-mindedness to challenge and revise our beliefs and patterns of self-talk, fostering personal growth and development.

The next exercise is aimed to encourage reflection on what factors have contributed to shaping your beliefs overall.

What messages did you receive about yourself when you were growing up? Were they overall positive or negative?

____

____

____

Can you identify any of them which you still believe today?

____

____

____

Can you think of a time when you adopted a belief about yourself based on what others thought or said about you?

____

____

____

____

____

Can you think of experiences in your life that have influenced the way you think about your abilities and potential?

____

____

____

____

____

Can you think of any instances where your beliefs about yourself were challenged and changed?

____

____

____

____

How did this impact your self-talk and behavior?

____

____

____

What, do you think, has been the biggest influence in your life which has shaped the beliefs you have about yourself and which you still hold today?

____

____

____

Have you ever questioned this biggest influence? Write down why.

____

____

____

Beliefs about Myself

Our beliefs about ourselves are the driving force behind our actions. These beliefs shape our decisions and guide our behavior. The outcomes we experience in our lives are a direct reflection of the actions we take, which are rooted in our beliefs. Our self-beliefs serve as the foundation of our life's journey. Without a particular belief about ourselves, we are unlikely to engage in related activities. For example, if I hold the belief that I'm not proficient in public speaking, I will likely shy away from such opportunities. Conversely, if I possess the belief that I am a skilled communicator, I will readily accept invitations to social events. Every action we undertake is fundamentally influenced by our core beliefs, whether they are positive or negative. This prompts us to consider: **What if some of these core beliefs are flawed? What if we let go of limiting beliefs? How might this transformation influence the actions we take and the outcomes we achieve in our lives?**

Case-study
Breaking Free from the Perfection Myth

Ben's's upbringing instilled in him a powerful belief: "You have to be the best to succeed." Raised in a family that emphasized relentless pursuit of excellence, Ben carried this mantra into adulthood. For years, he believed that anything less than perfection equated to failure.

As an adult, Ben's life was marked by unrelenting stress and anxiety. His pursuit of perfection had taken a toll on his mental and emotional well-being. During a moment of introspection, he began to question whether this deeply ingrained belief, instilled since childhood, was serving him well.

He embarked on a journey of self-reflection, observing successful individuals in various domains. He discovered that not all achievers were unparalleled experts in their fields. Many were distinguished by their dedication, resilience, and capacity for continuous improvement. It was then that Ben had a revelation: the notion of being the best was not an absolute prerequisite for success.

He decided to recalibrate his approach to life. He retained his commitment to excellence but shed the paralyzing fear of falling short of perfection. This transformative shift allowed him to tackle more ambitious projects, embrace failure as a learning opportunity, and expand his horizons. In his professional realm, he undertook endeavors he once deemed too risky and began mentoring others based on his experiences.

Over time, Ben experienced remarkable progress in his career. He evolved into a respected leader in his industry. Yet, beyond professional achievements, he experienced a profound sense of contentment and fulfillment. He realized that the belief he had harbored since childhood, while well-intentioned, had inadvertently held back his potential and subjected him to unnecessary stress.

Ben's journey serves as a testament to the power of challenging and altering limiting beliefs. Sometimes, letting go of deeply ingrained mantras from the past can open doors to greater success and personal happiness.

Case-study
From Silent Fear to Confident Speech

Judith was an exceptional writer. From her early years, she had a profound love for words and their ability to create captivating stories. However, despite her talent, there was a crippling fear that held her back from fully embracing her gift – a fear of public speaking.

The roots of this fear could be traced back to her childhood. Judith grew up in a household where the adage "children should be seen but not heard" was etched in stone. In a disciplined environment where voicing one's opinion was only permissible when requested by her parents, she learned to keep her thoughts locked away. The notion of speaking out became foreign and unsettling to her.

As the years passed, Judith's fear of speaking out evolved into an overwhelming dread of public speaking. The mere thought of addressing a crowd sent shivers down her spine. This fear had been a constant companion, lurking in the shadows of her success as a writer.

One day, as one of her books gained popularity, the local bookstore reached out to her. They requested her presence at a book event, where she would be expected to speak a few words about her work before the book signing. The invitation both excited and terrified her. The excitement stemmed from the recognition of her success as a writer, but the bitter aftertaste of her deep-seated fear of public speaking lingered.

Determined to overcome this obstacle, Judith sat down with pen and paper, to dig into this fear. She began by questioning herself, asking why she couldn't speak in public. Her initial response was a negative self-doubt: "I'm not capable of public speaking". She delved deeper and recognized that her fear had its roots in her upbringing. She modified her statement, acknowledging the influence of her past: "My fear of public speaking is because of my upbringing, but it's not my fault".

She wondered whether she could overcome this fear and wrote down "I have the potential to become a confident speaker because my past doesn't define who I am now. I am no longer a child, requesting permission to give my opinion. I am an adult, a successful author. I know that I can be a confident and engaging speaker."

Every day, in anticipation of her book signing event, Judith started practicing the mantra 'I can be a confident and engaging speaker' . Gradually she started feeling comfortable saying these words to herself. She started to accept the possibility that she could convey an interesting message that would engage her audience, just as she was doing with her books.

On the day of the event, she commenced with a pounding heart as she addressed her fans. Initially, she stuttered as she became aware of the gathered crowd looking at her. She felt a hot surge rising to her face. However, she persevered. She talked about her book, where she had got the idea from and the reasons for writing it. As her fans engaged more and started to ask her questions about her book, her nervousness began to ease allowing for her passion for writing to shine through. She could talk endlessly about her book. This was a pivotal moment in her life. The passion she had for writing overshadowed and transformed her fear of public speaking.

These days, Judith eagerly anticipates invitations from bookstores, where she wholeheartedly engages in crafting lively and captivating presentations to share with her fans during her book signing speeches.

Our deepest fears can be confronted and conquered. By challenging the beliefs through introspection, questioning and realization, we can transform our lives and achieve our full potential.

Write down beliefs about yourself that you wish to change.

Self-awareness in Decision-Making

Our brains are naturally wired to process information in ways that can lead to thinking and decision-making errors. For instance, we often have a tendency to seek information that confirms our existing beliefs rather than considering evidence that challenges them. Additionally, we may rely on easily accessible or memorable information rather than taking the time to gather more comprehensive or accurate data. These cognitive biases can significantly impact the way we perceive ourselves and the world, often resulting in inaccurate judgments or decisions.

When you practice awareness of your information-gathering methods, you may begin to recognize previously unconscious patterns of thinking and biases. By questioning your assumptions and beliefs, you become more open to exploring information beyond your usual sources, leading to greater self-awareness and self-knowledge. This self-awareness serves as a valuable foundation for personal growth and achieving excellence.

To cultivate awareness, take a step back and reflect on your decision-making processes. Consider how you gather information and the factors that influence your thinking. Be proactive in seeking alternative perspectives and evidence that challenge your assumptions, remaining receptive to new information. This practice will empower you to make more informed decisions and develop a nuanced understanding of complex issues.

The following exercise aims to help you compare your decision-making approaches in two contrasting situations: one where you believed you made the right decision and benefited from it, and another where you later regretted your choice. Analyze your thought processes, the factors you prioritized in each decision, and your main focus during those moments.

Think of a significant decision that you made in the past and which you later regretted. What were the factors which you based your decision on?

____

____

____

____

____

____

Why did you regret that decision later?

____

____

____

____

____

Recall and write down the beliefs you had about the situation (and/or person) and the self-talk that accompanied them.

Write down the assumptions you made about the situation (and/or person).

Can you identify a pattern of self-talk when taking that decision?

Consider the following before answering: there may be common themes such as (i) being overly criticial, (ii) jumping to conclusions, (iii) seeing it bigger than it actually is/was, (iv) making wrong assumptions, (v) a firm belief that something was true, (vi) intolerant, (vii) having fear (different types), (viii) feelings of doubt and uncertainty, (ix) not really knowing what you want, (x) feeling attacked. This list is not exhaustive and you may identify others during your reflection.

____

____

____

____

____

____

____

____

____

Now, think of a significant decision, made in the past, from which you positively reaped benefits, or are still enjoying those benefits.

Write down the beliefs you held surrounding the situation (and/or person) and the self-talk that you engaged in.

What were the negative aspects of the situation? Reflect on this and try to establish whether there were any which you ignored or believed were unimportant. Also decide whether you believe that you took a risk and state your reasons.

If you believe that there were no risks or that there were no negative aspects to this situation, I encourage you to find some. Then write down the probable decision that you would have taken, had you focused mostly on the negative aspects and ignored mostly the positive ones.

____

____

____

____

What aspects of the situation did you mostly focus on in taking this decision? Consider also the anticipations and assumptions that you made about the situation.

____

____

____

____

Judge your Answers: my informed conclusions

Now look back at the two decisions. How did your approach and mindset to each of these decisions vary? By identifying the difference in mindset between the two decisions, you can start to recognize what kind of impact your approach can have on the outcome of a decision.

Chapter 4
Taking Action
Challenging, Reframing, De-emphasizing, Prioritizing Me

It is now time to commit and take action to conquer your negative self-talk. In the first three chapters of this workbook we delved into the background work which is required to identify negative self-talk: practicing awareness and understanding what thoughts you give attention to is crucial. Taking your time to reflect on what triggers your negative self-talk and becoming aware of the beliefs that you hold about yourself are also important steps that cannot be skipped because they give you an understanding of the roots of your negative self-talk. If you have completed the previous chapters you are now ready to take real action to get rid of your negative self-talk forever.

In this chapter, we will explore specific strategies to eradicate negative self-talk and build a stronger sense of self-worth and self-esteem. Through these strategies, you will learn to break the cycle of negative self-talk and build a more positive and empowering inner dialogue. Here is a list of strategies that we will be exploring together:

1. **Challenging your Negative Self-Talk:** together we will question the validity of your negative self-talk and examine the evidence that contradicts it.
2. **Reframing your Negative Self-Talk:** there are many ways to perceive a situation. We will engage in scrutinizing a situation or a thought by looking at it from a different perspective.
3. **De-emphasizing your Negative Self-Talk**: we train our minds to consciously filter your self-talk de-emphasizing the negative and giving more attention to the positive.
4. **Prioritizing Me**: this exercise is about prioritizing yourself, your goals and dreams, your well-being, self-love and self-compassion.

Thoughts and Facts

Our thoughts, as a rule, aren't set in stone; they're not irrefutable facts. It's crucial to confront them head-on, subjecting them to critical examination regarding their accuracy and validity. When those negative thoughts creep in, ask yourself, 'Is this thought grounded in fact or merely an assumption?' and 'What evidence exists to substantiate this thought?' Picture your closest friend entangled in the same web of self-doubt. What words of encouragement and support would you offer them? This approach to tackling your negative self-talk can usher in significant enhancements to your self-esteem and overall well-being.

As we embark on the journey of questioning our negative self-talk, a remarkable transformation unfolds. We begin to discern the flaws within our pessimistic narrative. The realization dawns that this self-sabotaging chatter serves no constructive purpose. It doesn't fuel our motivation or act as a shield against potential failures or rejections. Instead, it's a recurring habit—a habit that can be swapped out for another. This marks the opportune moment for action, the moment when we gradually substitute those detrimental thoughts with more constructive and empowering ones.

Redefining the role of negative self-talk in our lives entails acknowledging its inherent lack of value. Through the process of challenging and reframing these negative thoughts, we embark on a journey toward a more optimistic and empowering internal dialogue. This healthier inner dialogue becomes the driving force behind our pursuit of goals, our resilience in the face of adversity, our self-compassion amidst mistakes, and our ability to forge stronger, more fulfilling relationships.

Think about a recent event where your initial thoughts about it were later proven to be inaccurate or incomplete. How did this experience highlight the difference between thoughts and facts?

But what if, what I believe is true?

As you delved into the previous section, you might have found yourself engaged in an internal dialogue, perhaps pondering, 'What if the things I tell myself are actually true? What if I truly am prone to messing things up? What if I'm genuinely not good enough?'

Doubts are a part of the human experience. So, let's entertain the idea—what if it's true that you made a mistake? So what? Can you have this conversation with yourself? **'So what? Yes, I made an error, but I won't dwell on it more than necessary to understand how I can improve. Moreover, I won't allow one slip to define my future performance.'**

Recognizing that making mistakes is entirely acceptable is paramount. It's also crucial, sometimes in hindsight, to acknowledge that your negative self-talk might have blown the situation out of proportion. Negative self-talk can arise from various sources, including past negative experiences, external circumstances, and our own cognitive biases. It's entirely plausible that this internal chatter doesn't accurately reflect who you are or what you're capable of achieving.

Alternatively, when you catch yourself thinking, 'What if it's true?' or 'What if I'm simply not good enough?' consider confronting these thoughts directly. Challenge them by asking if they hold true in all situations where you've made mistakes. Were you solely responsible? Can you recall instances where you've excelled or achieved your goals? Is there at least one valuable lesson you've gained from this mistake or failure?

Kindness and compassion are virtues we often extend to others but withhold from ourselves. Isn't it somewhat absurd? If you would readily offer your best friend, another human being, the kindness, compassion, and understanding they deserve, then why wouldn't you afford the same to yourself? After all, you too are a human being and a friend to yourself.

Are you a friend to yourself?

Take a moment and reflect on this question. Examine whether you offer yourself the same compassion, understanding and encouragement that you readily give to your best friend.

Has anyone close to you challenged a negative belief that you held about yourself? Reflect on their perspective and the alternative view they held. Did you accept their view? Give your reasons.

Chellenging Negative Self-Talk

When we find ourselves in a negative situation, our perception often becomes skewed, leading to distorted beliefs about ourselves and our circumstances. We have a tendency to magnify our weaknesses and dwell on our shortcomings, resulting in harsh self-criticism. We may catastrophize or exaggerate the situation's negative aspects and we often ignore our strengths and accomplishments.

The next exercise will allow you to step out of the situation and examine it more objectively. It will encourage you to challenge your negative self-talk and to look for evidence which supports a more balanced and realistic perspective about the situation and yourself.

Here are the strategies we will practice to effectively challenge our negative self-talk:

1. **Seeking Evidence: Finding evidence in your life that shows that your statement is not absolutely true.**
2. **Personalization Check: Checking in with yourself to see if you are taking things too personally.**
3. **External Factors Check and Reality Check: Looking at external factors which may have contributed to the negative situation and Re-sizing it into a more realistic picture.**

The strategy you choose to use will vary depending on the nature of the negative statement you wish to challenge. Some statements may align with a single specific strategy, while others might benefit from the application of multiple strategies among these three options. The upcoming exercises will help you identify the specific strategy required to effectively challenge your negative self-talk statements.

1. Seeking Evidence

<u>This strategy is most effective when applied to your own self-beliefs, covering aspects like your personality, appearance, intelligence, and capabilities.</u> Below you'll find a list of common negative self-talk statements to help you get started. Alternatively you may wish to go back to page where you reflected on beliefs about yourself that you would like to change

- "I'm not good enough."
- "I'll never succeed."
- "I always mess things up."
- "I'm such a failure."
- "I can't do it."
- "Nobody likes me."
- "I'm so stupid."
- "I'll never be happy."
- "I don't deserve good things."
- "I'm worthless."
- "I'm a burden to others."
- "I'll never be as good as them."
- "I'm too fat/skinny/ugly."
- "I'll never be successful."
- "I'm always the victim."
- "I'm a failure in everything I do."
- "No one cares about me."
- "I'm destined to be alone."
- "I'll never get ahead in life."
- "I'm just not talented enough."
- "I'm always overlooked."
- "I'll never be as good as others expect me to be."
- "I'm such a disappointment."
- "I don't belong anywhere."
- "I'll never achieve my dreams."

Choose a statement from the list you wrote in Chapter 3, on page   , or use the provided list, to complete this exercise.

My statement: ____

____

Is this statement absolutely true? Can you identify an instance in your life that contradicts this statement? Write down all the important details about this particular life instance. Include the circumstances and your thoughts and feelings.

____

____

____

____

Re-write your chosen statement followed by a new sentence beginning with 'However', e.g. *"I am ugly. However, ..."*, *"I'll never succeed. However, ..."*.

____

____

____

____

Write down the opposite of your chosen statement:

____

____

How does this statement make me feel?

____

____

Find three positive aspects in your personality and complete the sentence by using 'because', _e.g. I am a very caring person because I always lend an ear to my friends and do my best to help them out._

____

____

____

____

Write down three things that you can do every day to remind yourself about your positive qualities.

____

____

____

2. Personalization Check

In Chapter 1, we delved into the importance of 'awareness.' How conscious are you of whether you tend to internalize criticism, rejection, or failure? The following quiz is designed to assist you in gauging whether you have a tendency to take things personally or not. Recognizing such a tendency will enable you to take a step back and assess unwanted situations more objectively, armed with the knowledge that you may tend to internalize them personally.

1. When someone criticizes my work, I often feel like it's a personal attack.

Frequently

Rarely

Sometimes

2. Rejection makes me question whether I did something wrong.

Frequently

Rarely

Sometimes

3. Failure makes me doubt whether I am really capable.

Frequently

Rarely

Sometimes

4. I don't expect positive and successful situations to happen to me.

Frequently

Rarely

Sometimes

5. I knew this would happen to me.

Frequently

Rarely

Sometimes

Reflection

Let's delve into your results to better understand your attitudes and how they can shape your overall mindset.

1. When someone criticizes my work, I often feel like it's a personal attack.

- **Frequently**: You tend to take criticism personally most of the time. It may be beneficial to work on developing a thicker skin and not internalizing criticism as much.
- **Rarely**: You generally don't take criticism personally, which is a healthy mindset. You likely view criticism as constructive feedback rather than a personal attack.
- **Sometimes**: You have a moderate tendency to take criticism personally. It's worth exploring why this happens on occasion and working on strategies to address it.

2. Rejection makes me question whether I did something wrong.

- **Frequently**: You often perceive rejection as a reflection of your actions. It's important to remember that rejection can occur for various reasons, and it's not always related to your actions.
- **Rarely**: You typically don't link rejection to personal wrongdoing, which is a positive attitude. You likely understand that rejection can result from numerous factors.
- **Sometimes**: You occasionally connect rejection to your actions. It's useful to investigate when and why this happens.

Notes:

____

____

____

____

3. Failure makes me doubt whether I am really capable.

- **Frequently:** You frequently doubt your capabilities when you encounter failure. It's essential to recognize that everyone experiences failures, and they don't define your overall capabilities.
- **Rarely:** You usually don't let failure undermine your belief in your capabilities, which is a resilient attitude. You likely see failures as opportunities for growth.
- **Sometimes:** You sometimes question your capabilities after a failure. Identifying when and why this occurs can help you build a more robust self-belief.

4. I don't expect positive and successful situations to happen to me.

- **Frequently:** You often have low expectations for positive outcomes in your life. It might be beneficial to work on cultivating a more optimistic outlook.
- **Rarely:** You typically have optimistic expectations for positive outcomes, which is a healthy mindset. This attitude can enhance your overall well-being.
- **Sometimes:** You occasionally have low expectations for success. Exploring the situations or circumstances when this happens can be insightful for personal growth.

5. I knew this would happen to me.

- **Frequently:** You often anticipate negative outcomes in advance. It's valuable to challenge this negative anticipation and explore more positive possibilities.
- **Rarely:** You generally don't have negative anticipations about outcomes, which is a positive outlook. You likely approach situations with an open mind.
- **Sometimes:** You occasionally anticipate negative outcomes. Identifying when and why you do this can help you develop a more constructive mindset.

The Right Attitude

Let's review the five questions from the quiz and explore the optimal attitudes for maintaining a healthy mindset in each of these scenarios.

1. When someone criticizes my work, I often feel like it's a personal attack.

1. When someone criticizes my work, I see it as an opportunity for constructive feedback and growth.
2. Instead of taking criticism personally, I focus on separating my work from my self-worth.
3. I believe that feedback, even if negative, can help me improve and achieve my goals.
4. I understand that not everyone will agree with or appreciate my work, and that's okay.
5. I view criticism as a chance to learn and develop, rather than as a reflection of my value as a person.

2. Rejection makes me question whether I did something wrong.

1. Rejection helps me reflect on my actions and consider areas for improvement.
2. Instead of assuming I did something wrong, I look for other factors that might have contributed to the rejection.
3. I see rejection as a redirection towards opportunities that are better suited for me.
4. I recognize that rejection is a natural part of life and doesn't define my worth.
5. I use rejection as motivation to persevere and prove my capabilities.

3. Failure makes me doubt whether I am really capable.

1. Failure is a chance for me to learn and grow, not a reflection of my overall capabilities.
2. Instead of doubting myself, I focus on what I can improve to achieve success next time.
3. I see failure as an essential step on the path to success, not as a sign of incompetence.
4. I know that even the most successful people have faced failure, and it's part of the journey.
5. I use failure as an opportunity to build resilience and determination.

4. I don't expect positive and successful situations to happen to me.

1. I believe in my ability to create positive and successful situations in my life.
2. I approach life with a positive outlook, expecting good things to come my way.
3. I understand that my attitude and actions play a significant role in attracting positive outcomes.
4. I actively work towards my goals and believe in my potential to achieve them.
5. I embrace opportunities with confidence, knowing that I can turn them into successful experiences.

5. I knew this would happen to me.

1. I acknowledge that setbacks and challenges are a part of life, and I'm prepared to face them.
2. I view unexpected events as opportunities for growth and learning.
3. I stay resilient in the face of adversity and look for solutions to overcome obstacles.
4. I maintain a positive attitude even when things don't go as planned.
5. I understand that life is full of surprises, and I'm open to the possibilities they bring.

3. External Factors Check and Reality Check

<u>Strategy 3 is most effective when applied to negative self-talk statements that stem from negative or unwanted situations.</u>

Below, you'll find a list of common negative self-talk statements that often arise in such cases.

1. "I knew I'd fail; I'm a failure."
2. "Nobody likes me; I must be unlikeable."
3. "I can't do anything right."
4. "I'll never recover from this rejection."
5. "I'm just not good enough."
6. "I should have seen this criticism coming."
7. "I'll never be able to face them again."
8. "I'll never succeed; it's impossible."
9. "I'm so stupid for making that mistake."
10. "I'm a disappointment to everyone."
11. "They were right; I'm worthless."
12. "I'll never be able to prove myself."
13. "I'll never be respected."
14. "I don't deserve success."
15. "I'll always be a loser."
16. "I'm just a burden to others."
17. "I should have done better; I'm a failure."
18. "I'll never be able to live this down."
19. "I'll never be able to recover from this criticism."
20. "I'm a complete and utter failure."
21. "I'll never be able to face them again."
22. "I'll always be a disappointment."
23. "I'll never amount to anything."
24. "I'm unworthy of love and respect."
25. "I'm a total failure in life."

Choose a statement from the list or use your own, to complete this exercise.

My statement: ____

____

Describe the situation where you said this statement to yourself.

____

____

____

____

Can you identify external factors that were beyond your control, in this situation? What were they, and how did they contribute to the outcome?

____

____

____

____

Were there any other people involved whose actions or decisions influenced the situation? How did their actions play a role?

____

____

____

____

Consider what aspects of the situation, if any, were within your control or influence. Were there any choices or actions you took that contributed to the outcome?

____

____

____

____

Reflect on whether it's fair to place the entire blame on yourself for this situation. Why or why not?

____

____

Imagine looking at this situation from a broader perspective. How might your perception change if you viewed it as a temporary setback rather than a permanent failure?

Can you identify any lessons or opportunities for growth that this situation might offer if viewed differently?

Are there alternative viewpoints or narratives that could help you see this situation in a more realistic and less negative light?

Consider how exploring these aspects of the situation makes you feel. Has your perspective on the situation evolved? Do you feel differently about your role in it?

Reframing Negative Self-Talk

When life serves us with unwanted situations or when we stumble upon a grave mistake, we possess a remarkable ability - the power to choose how we interpret these moments. Successful individuals often harness this power to maintain their self-love, nurture self-compassion, and stay aligned with their goals and dreams.

Reframing negative self-talk is a conscious practice rooted in heightened self-awareness. **It's a realization that you no longer want to inflict mental suffering upon yourself.** Instead, it's a commitment to empowering your mind. It involves replacing negative mental statements with ones that are positive and balanced. This act of self-empowerment is more than just positive thinking; it's a pathway to taking meaningful actions that enhance your overall life.

This practice fosters the development of emotional resilience and inner strength. It equips you with the resolve to tackle challenges, bounce back from setbacks, and navigate stress with grace. Reframing is your toolkit for maintaining a healthier mindset, paving the way to a more fulfilled and successful life.

Understanding the concept of reframing negative self-talk is one thing, but the real magic happens when you put it into practice. In the following exercise, I'll provide you with several examples of common negative self-talk statements. We'll walk through the process of reframing each statement together, but here's an important tip: I strongly encourage you to do this exercise in writing.

Why? Because when you write down your thoughts and actively engage in the process of reframing on paper, it has a powerful impact on your brain. Writing helps solidify the changes in perception and belief, making them more ingrained in your thought patterns. It's a tangible way to rewire your thinking, and the benefits can be transformative.

As we work through these examples together, remember that reframing is a skill that becomes more effective with practice.

Negative Self-Talk: "I can't believe I messed up that presentation. I'm such a failure. I'll never be good at public speaking."

Reframed Self-Talk: "I had a challenging moment during the presentation, but everyone makes mistakes sometimes. This is an opportunity for me to learn and improve my public speaking skills. I can seek feedback and practice to get better."

In this example, the negative self-talk initially focuses on the mistake and generalizes it to mean failure in public speaking. The reframed self-talk acknowledges the mistake but shifts the focus to a growth mindset. It recognizes that making mistakes is part of the learning process and emphasizes the opportunity for improvement.

Steps:
1. *Identify the negative statement*
2. *Reframe it : (i) include a constructive perspective*
         (ii) include a growth oriented perspective.

Further Examples

Negative Self-Talk: "I can't believe I gained weight. I'm so unattractive."

Reframed Self-Talk: "I've noticed some changes in my weight, but my worth isn't determined by my appearance alone. I can focus on leading a healthier lifestyle."

Negative Self-Talk: "I'll never find a job. I'm just not good enough."

Reframed Self-Talk: "Job searching can be tough, but I have valuable skills and experiences. I'll keep applying and improving my resume and interview skills."

Negative Self-Talk: "I made a fool of myself at the party. I'm so awkward."

Reframed Self-Talk: "I may have had an off moment, but everyone does sometimes. I can choose to focus on the enjoyable parts of the evening."

Negative Self-Talk: "I'm overwhelmed by my workload. I'll never get it all done."

Reframed Self-Talk: "I have a lot on my plate, but I can break tasks into smaller steps and prioritize. I've handled busy periods before."

Practice Reframing

Use the space below to practice reframing your negative self-talk. Start by identifying your habitual negative self-talk statements and write them all down. Then proceed to tackle them one by one. A helpful question to ask yourself is: How can I reframe this thought in a more positive and balanced way? What constructive statement can I use for this negative statement? How can I grow in this?

Practice this exercise regularly. More templates like the ones below can be found on page 166. Over time, you'll strengthen your ability to reframe and replace negative self-talk and it will become your default mindset.

Negative Self-Talk:

Reframed Self-Talk:

Negative Self-Talk:

Reframed Self-Talk:

De-emphasizing Negative Self -Talk

We now delve into a powerful technique: de-emphasizing. **This strategy is most effective when you blame yourself for a negative outcome within a given situation.**

De-emphasizing is about diminishing the impact of negative self-talk by consciously giving it less importance. Instead of engaging in a battle of wits with your inner critic, you'll focus on finding silver linings and positive aspects in the situations that trigger negative thoughts.

De-emphasizing negative self-talk is, at its core, about shifting your main point of focus. It involves a process of transformation, taking a statement with a negative self-judgment and gradually moving it towards a positive future outlook.

De-emphasizing doesn't mean ignoring your feelings or pretending that everything is perfect. It's a method for shifting your perspective and fostering resilience in the face of adversity. By consciously choosing to downplay negative self-talk, you allow space for a more balanced and constructive view to emerge.

Let's break this process down:

1. **Recognize your self-criticism and write it down:** If you have practiced awareness in Chapter 1, you are now able to recognize when your negative self-talk creeps in. Acknowledge the emotions that you are feeling or that you felt at the time. This is a crucial step because it validates your feelings without surrendering to self-criticism. Write down your negative statement.

2. **Transform the statement into a neutral one:** Remove the self-judgment from your statement, turning it into a neutral one. For example, "I really messed up my studies this semester," reframe it to "My studies are not where I wish them to be." This neutral statement removes self-judgment and creates a platform for positive change.

3. **Add a future positive statement to it:** Finally, add a positive future-oriented statement to your self-talk. In our example, it could become "In the future I will actively work to improve my studies and achieve my goals." This positive statement emphasizes future growth and potential.

4. **Taking Action:** Give an answer to **"What action can I take to make this happen?"** In the same example, the statement would be "I will make a reasonable schedule of studies which is easy for me to stick to". In this last step of the process, you will be providing yourself a clear and actionable plan to implement your future positive statement.

At this stage, it's important to recognize that the goal isn't solely about immediate commitment to a specific plan of action. While taking concrete steps toward positive change is valuable, this exercise also serves a vital purpose in training your mind. It's an opportunity to expand your mental horizons and cultivate a mindset that remains open to various possibilities. By exploring different avenues and potential actions, you're nurturing your ability to adapt, innovate, and consider alternative paths.

Here are a few examples to help you get started with practicing de-emphasizing.

Practicing De-emphasizing

Self-Criticism: "I can't believe I ate that entire cake. I'm such a failure."

Neutral Statement: "That cake was too good not to be eaten entirely."

Positive Future Statement: "I'll balance indulgence with healthier choices."

What action can I take to make this happen? "I'll strive to eat healthy most days, so when I indulge, it's already balanced with my regular healthy eating."

Self-Criticism: "I always procrastinate and never meet deadlines."

Neutral Statement: "Meeting deadlines can be challenging for me."

Positive Future Statement: "I'm gradually improving my time management skills."

What action can I take to make this happen? "I will create a detailed task schedule at the beginning of each week. Everyday I will commit to working on tasks for a specific amount of time, ensuring that I make steady progress. By breaking tasks into smaller, manageable steps, I'll build momentum and improve my ability to meet deadlines consistently."

Self-Criticism: "I'm a terrible parent; I can't handle my child's behavior."

Neutral Statement: "I found it challenging to manage my child's behavior today."

Positive Future Statement: "I'm learning effective parenting strategies."

What action can I take to make this happen? "I will schedule an hour every week to read and learn about parenting strategies, and to start consistently applying what I learn and adapt it to my children's behavior."

Self-Criticism: "I can't believe I forgot our anniversary. I'm a terrible partner."

Neutral Statement: "I forgot our anniversary this year."

Positive Future Statement: "I'll make it up to my partner and be more attentive."

What action can I take to make this happen? "I will acknowledge and apologize for my oversight, plan a special date to make it up to my partner and get in the habit of setting up reminders for important dates."

Self-Criticism: "I'm terrible at managing my finances; I can't save money."

Neutral Statement: "My current financial situation doesn't include much savings."

Positive Future Statement: "I'm learning to manage my finances better and build a strong savings habit."

What action can I take to make this happen? "I will create a budget, track my expenses, and allocate a portion of my income to savings each month, even if it means giving up some of my indulgences."

Self-Criticism: "I'm terrible with technology; I can't keep up with new gadgets."

Neutral Statement: "I sometimes find it challenging to adapt to new technology."

Positive Future Statement: "I'm eager to learn and embrace technological advancements."

What action can I take to make this happen? "I will take online tech courses, explore new gadgets gradually, and seek help when needed to become more tech-savvy."

Practicing De-emphasizing

Use the following template to practice de-emphasizing in situations where you tend to blame yourself. *There are more templates like these for you to fill in and practice, starting at page 169.*

Self-Criticism: ____

____

____

Neutral Statement: ____

____

Positive Future Statement: ____

____

____

What action can I take to make this happen? ____

____

____

____

Prioritizing Me

"Do you know how precious you are? Can you take a moment to reflect on this simple but profound statement: '**I am precious in this world**.'

Have you ever considered that you are an essential component of this planet? That the Earth was created for you to live on, to experience, to love, to learn, and to achieve? Your worth is intrinsic and immeasurable. You bring a unique light to the world, a set of qualities, experiences, and dreams that belong to no one else but you.

This section is dedicated to you — to the seeker of self-acceptance, the dreamer of brighter tomorrows, and the believer in your own potential. It's a reminder that you have the capacity to transform negative self-talk into positive action, to turn self-doubt into self-compassion, and to cultivate a more profound love for yourself.

In this final section, we will embark on a journey of self-discovery, affirmations, mindfulness, and gratitude. You'll learn to recognize your strengths, visualize your dreams, and appreciate the beauty of life itself. And as you take these steps, always remember that you are precious, and your journey is worth celebrating."

Discovering the Positives Within

Let's begin by exploring the positives within you. We all have strengths and qualities that make us special, even though these aspects of ourselves might sometimes get overshadowed by self-doubt or negative self-talk.

Reflect on yourself, as a person and **highlight** any of these positive qualities that you identify in yourself and that family and friends have identified in you.

My Qualities

reliability

resourcefulness

friendliness

kindness

curiosity

generosity

empathy

honesty

integrity

patience

compassion

courage

gratitude

resilience

altruism

forgiveness

graciousness

perseverence

humility

caring

creativity

tolerance

courteousness

open-mindedness

imagination

diligence

self-discipline

leadership

Self-Appreciation Letter

Now that you've taken the time to identify and highlight your positive qualities, it's time to celebrate and appreciate yourself even more. I would like you to write a self-appreciation letter to acknowledge your worth and your unique qualities, that make you who you are.

Find a quiet place where you feel cozy and comfortable and begin with expressing gratitude to yourself, reflecting on the positive qualities that you possess. Be specific and mention each quality that you possess and explain why it is valuable to you and others. Share examples of how you've demonstrated these qualities.

Now, reflect on your accomplishments, no matter how big or small. This could be personal growth, a realization, professional success or any area of your life where you've made progress.

Next, write about your intentions to continue nurturing and expressing these qualities. Set positive intentions for how you'll use these qualities in the future to enhance your life and the lives of those around you.

Finally, end your letter with a note of love, encouragement, and appreciation for yourself. Remind yourself that you are deserving of self-love and self-compassion.

Once you've completed your self-appreciation letter, keep it in a safe and accessible place. You can revisit it whenever you need a reminder of your worth and positive qualities.

Embrace this process, and let your self-appreciation letter be a source of inspiration and encouragement on your journey to greater self-acceptance and well-being.

Letter to Myself

Dear

Gratitude

____

____

____

Accomplishments

____

____

____

Intentions

____

____

____

____

With love and appreciation,

The Positive in My Life

Our lives are comprised of countless facets, often teeming with positivity that we inadvertently overlook while dwelling on what could be improved. Cultivating inner positivity and peace begins with recognizing and cherishing the goodness in our external environment.

In the following exercise, our attention will be directed towards various dimensions of our lives, illuminating the positive elements that enrich our existence and enhance our comfort. This is a journey of reflection and appreciation, an opportunity to open our eyes to the bountiful blessings in our lives. Whether it's the warmth of affection and friendship, the support and kindness we receive from others, the comfort of our homes, or the steady flow of income, no matter how grand or modest, all contribute to our well-being. We will dedicate ourselves to uncovering the most positive aspects across 12 key areas of our lives and expressing our gratitude and appreciation.

Appreciation and gratitude are not just fleeting feelings; they are powerful forces that can transform our perspective and enhance our well-being. By taking the time to acknowledge and give thanks for the positive elements in our lives, we not only foster a sense of contentment and happiness, but we also cultivate resilience and mental strength. This exercise is essential for maintaining our mental health because it reminds us that even in the midst of challenges, there is a wealth of goodness surrounding us. It teaches us to see life through a lens of abundance rather than scarcity, and it allows us to approach each day with a grateful heart, ready to embrace the beauty and positivity that exists in the world around us.

Before embarking on this exercise, take a few moments to center yourself. Focus on your breath, inhaling and exhaling deeply, grounding yourself in the present moment.

What Am I Grateful for?

My Family

My Friends

My Personal Growth

My Career

What Am I Grateful for?

My Health and Welness

My Romantic Relationships

My Social Life

My Spiritual Life

What Am I Grateful for?

My Hobbies and Interests

My Community

My Finances

My Home

Dream Big

It is now time to channel the positivity that you have built in the previous exercises, toward your dreams.

The dreams you hold within you are the seeds of your potential. They represent what's truly possible when you believe in yourself.

In this next exercise, we're going to delve into your aspirations for the future, using the power of both writing and visualization. Through this process, you'll not only define your dreams but also breathe life into them in the theater of your mind. This exercise will help you connect with your deepest desires, boost your self-esteem, and give you a profound sense of purpose.

We will first begin by practicing visualization. You'll need to find a quiet area where you can connect with yourself and allow your imagination to flow. Visualization will allow you to see and feel your dreams clearly in your mind, making them more tangible and achievable.

We will then move on to identifying your bucket list, dreams, and aspirations for the future and write about them in vivid detail, exploring the emotions they stir within us.

Find a quiet and comfortable place. Take a few deep breaths to relax and close your eyes. Spend a minute focusing on your breath. You are now ready to embark on this journey of self-discovery and empowerment.

Practicing Visualization

Read each statement, then close your eyes and vividly imagine it in your mind's eye. Create a clear mental image of the scenario and concentrate on the sensations you would experience if you were actually there. Pay attention to:

- **The detailed picture you see in your mind.**
- **The scents wafting through the air.**
- **The sounds filling your ears.**
- **The physical sensations coursing through your body.**
- **The emotions that this scenario evokes in you.**

Once you have a comprehensive mental image enriched with all these sensations, jot them down. Do one exercise daily for the next 6 days.

Imagine standing in a lush forest on a crisp autumn morning. Describe what you see, the sounds that you hear, the smell in the air and the sensations that you feel in your body.

____

____

____

____

____

How does it feel to be in this forest?

____

____

Imagine biting into a juicy, ripe fruit. Describe the taste, the texture, and the aroma of the fruit.

____

____

____

How does it make you feel?

____

____

Imagine that you are on a sandy beach on a hot summer day, dipping your feet in the cool ocean. Describe the sensations that you feel on your feet.

____

____

____

Describe the sensations that you feel on your skin.

____

____

How does this make you feel?

____

Imagine walking through a bustling, colorful market in a foreign city. Describe the vibrant sights, the exotic scents, and the sounds of people haggling.

____

____

____

What is one thing that strikes you in this scenario?

____

____

Imagine sitting by a crackling fireplace on a snowy winter evening. Describe the room that you are in.

____

____

____

Describe how the environment makes you feel.

____

____

____

Imagine that you are having dinner with your dream partner. Describe the restaurant that you are in.

____

____

How does the environment around you feel?

____

____

What are you wearing?

____

____

What is your partner saying to you?

____

____

How does your partner make you feel?

____

____

My Bucket List

Spend a moment contemplating your bucket list. Here's a list to kickstart your thoughts, but feel free to jot down your own ideas in the provided space.

- **Travel to every continent.**
- **Skydiving or parachuting.**
- **Visit the Seven Wonders of the World.**
- **Go on a hot air balloon ride.**
- **Learn a new language.**
- **Take a cross-country road trip.**
- **Swim with dolphins.**
- **Write a book or screenplay.**
- **See the Northern Lights.**
- **Volunteer for a charitable cause.**
- **Go on a wildlife safari.**
- **Learn to play a musical instrument.**
- **Take a cruise.**
- **Attend a major music or film festival.**
- **Climb a famous mountain.**
- **Learn to surf or scuba dive.**
- **Take a ride on the Orient Express.**
- **Explore an ancient ruin.**
- **Attend the Olympics.**
- **Go on a spiritual retreat.**
- **Take a helicopter tour.**

- Experience zero gravity.
- Attend a major sports event.
- Go on a luxury spa retreat.
- Achieve a personal fitness or health goal.
- Learn a new cooking skill or recipe.
- Take a photography course.
- Complete a home renovation project.
- Volunteer regularly at a local charity or nonprofit.
- Run a 5k or participate in a charity walk.
- Plant a garden and watch it flourish.
- Start a regular exercise routine and stick to it.
- Attend a live theater performance or local play.
- Learn to dance.
- Write a letter to your future self.
- Take a scenic hike.
- Try meditation or yoga to reduce stress.
- Join a book club or reading group.
- Host a dinner party for friends or family.
- Take a weekend getaway.
- Learn basic car maintenance or repair.
- Attend a local music concert or small venue gig.
- Visit a museum or art gallery.
- Master a new craft or DIY hobby.
- Take up a new sport or physical activity.
- Start a collection.

My Bucket List

1

2

3

4

5

6

7

8

9

10

11

12

13

14

15

Defining My Dreams and Aspirations

Imagine your Ideal Future.

Close your eyes and imagine a future where everything you've ever dreamed of has come true. What does that world look like? Describe it in vivid detail, from your surroundings to your daily life.

Here is an example to get you started:

In my ideal future, I wake up to the gentle sounds of waves crashing on the shore. I'm living in a cozy beachfront cottage, surrounded by lush greenery and the ocean's endless horizon. My mornings start with yoga and meditation on the beach, followed by writing in my sunlit home office. I spend my afternoons working on projects I'm passionate about, like writing a book that's been in my heart for years. Evenings are for enjoying homemade dinners with loved ones and stargazing by the bonfire. It's a life filled with peace, creativity, and connection.

Big Dreams and Goals

Reflect on the big dreams and goals you've had for yourself. What are they, and why are they important to you?

Here is an example:

One of my most significant dreams is to become a published author. I've always had a deep love for storytelling, and I want to share my narratives with the world. I also dream of traveling extensively, experiencing different cultures, and capturing these journeys through my writing and photography.

Passion-Driven Aspirations

What ignites your passion? Imagine that you are immersed in this passion? Describe how it makes you feel?

Here is an example:

Dance is my ultimate passion. It's the fluidity of body movements that captivates me, the freedom and the lightness that I feel. It's not just about the steps; it's about graceful sways or fiery rhythms that allow me to express different states of mind. Dance allows me to express my sweet and romantic side, my aggressive side and robust side, and my attractiveness.

____

____

____

____

____

____

____

____

Visualize

Now, take a moment to visualize your future, your dreams and your passions. See yourself living the life you've always dreamed of, having the things you've always wanted and being immersed in your passions everyday.

Now write down the feelings that you have experienced during this visualization.

____

____

____

____

____

____

____

____

Do this exercise regularly. Tweak and change as you go along and be as specific as you can in your visualization. There are more templates for you to fill in and practice, starting at page 174.

Affirm

Think of statements that you can say to yourself daily that encourage you to follow your dreams and passions. Make it a daily practice, to read the ones that feel right to you. *On pages 179-183 you will find a set of affirmations that you may wish to cut out and affix somewhere prominent in your home, as a daily reminder.*

Here are a few statements to get you started.

- "I am taking small, consistent steps toward my dreams every day."

- "I believe in my abilities and the path I've chosen."

- "Obstacles are just opportunities to learn and grow on my journey."

- "I am committed to nurturing my passions and making them a priority."

- "My dreams are worth pursuing, and I am worth the effort."

- "I am open to new opportunities that align with my passions."

- "I trust the timing of my journey; everything happens for a reason."

- "I embrace failure as a stepping stone to success."

- "I am creating a life that reflects my deepest passions."

- "I find inspiration and motivation within myself every day."

Action Commitment

Select one of your dreams. Reflect on one specific action, no matter how small it is, that you can commit to taking today or in the near future to move closer to that dream. Write it down.

____

____

____

____

____

____

____

____

____

Engage in this exercise regularly to train your brain. Starting on page 185 you will find more templates like this, to practice your action commitment.

Conclusion

As we reach the final pages of this book, dear reader, I want you to take a moment to reflect on the incredible journey we've undertaken together. It's been a journey filled with introspection, self-discovery, and transformation **—a journey guided by the resolute belief that you are deserving of self-love, self-compassion, and the fulfillment of your deepest dreams.**

In this concluding chapter, we shifted our focus from the shadows of negative self-talk to the radiant light within. We sought to challenge, reframe, and de-emphasize the negativity that has held us captive for far too long. But this chapter was not just about combatting the darkness; it was a celebration of your worthiness, your dreams, and your boundless aspirations.

The exercises you've encountered here are not mere tasks to be completed and forgotten. They are, in fact, keys to an ongoing voyage of self-discovery and empowerment. Return to them as often as you desire, adjusting, improving, and allowing them to evolve alongside you.

With practice, these exercises will become a seamless part of your daily life. You'll find yourself less reliant on writing them down, as your mind will naturally gravitate toward self-love, self-compassion, and the pursuit of your dreams.

As you turn the final page and close this chapter of your life, remember this: You are a magnificent tapestry of experiences, dreams, and potential. The journey of conquering negative self-talk is not one that ends here—it is a lifelong expedition, and you are the intrepid explorer.

With every step you take, every word you speak, and every dream you pursue, carry the knowledge that you are capable of greatness. Empower yourself with the belief that your inner narrative can be rewritten, that self-doubt can be transformed into self-compassion, and that your life is a canvas waiting for your masterpiece.

Thank you for entrusting me to be your guide on this profound journey. As you continue your exploration of self-love and empowerment, know that you are never alone. The connection we've forged through these pages endures, and the wisdom you've gained will accompany you, lighting the path toward your most vibrant and empowered self.

Embrace the journey, for it is yours to conquer. Your adventure continues, and it's a story worth celebrating.

You're a STAR!

WELL DONE!

Dear reader,

Congratulations on completing "How to Conquer Negative Self-Talk." You've taken a significant step towards improving your self-talk and building a more positive mindset. I genuinely appreciate your trust in this workbook, and I'm grateful that you chose it to be part of your personal growth journey.

Your commitment to self-improvement is inspiring, and I hope you've found valuable insights and strategies within these pages to help you overcome negative self-talk. Your dedication to personal growth is a testament to your strength and determination.

If you found this workbook helpful and transformative, I kindly invite you to share your thoughts and experiences by leaving a review. Your feedback will not only help others discover the benefits of this workbook but also motivate and guide them on their path to conquering negative self-talk.

Thank you once again for choosing "How to Conquer Negative Self-Talk." I wish you continued success and a life filled with positivity, self-compassion, and inner strength.

Warm regards,

Natasha
xx

Templates for further practice

Negative Self-Talk:

Reframed Self-Talk:

Negative Self-Talk:

Reframed Self-Talk:

Negative Self-Talk:

Reframed Self-Talk:

Negative Self-Talk:

Reframed Self-Talk:

Negative Self-Talk:

Reframed Self-Talk:

Negative Self-Talk:

Reframed Self-Talk:

Negative Self-Talk:

Reframed Self-Talk:

Negative Self-Talk:

Reframed Self-Talk:

Negative Self-Talk:

Reframed Self-Talk:

Practicing De-emphasizing

Self-Criticism: _______________________________________

____

____

Neutral Statement: _______________________________________

____

Positive Future Statement: _______________________________________

____

____

What action can I take to make this happen? _______________________________________

____

____

____

Practicing De-emphasizing

Self-Criticism: _______________________________

____

____

Neutral Statement: _______________________________

____

Positive Future Statement: _______________________________

____

____

What action can I take to make this happen? _______________________________

____

____

____

Practicing De-emphasizing

Self-Criticism: _______________________________

____

____

Neutral Statement: _______________________________

____

Positive Future Statement: _______________________________

____

____

What action can I take to make this happen? _______________________________

____

____

____

Practicing De-emphasizing

Self-Criticism: _______________________________

____

____

Neutral Statement: _______________________________

____

Positive Future Statement: _______________________________

____

____

What action can I take to make this happen? _______________________________

____

____

____

Practicing De-emphasizing

Self-Criticism: _______________________________________

____

____

Neutral Statement: _______________________________

____

Positive Future Statement: _______________________

____

____

What action can I take to make this happen? ________

____

____

____

Visualization Practice

Take a moment to visualize one of your greatest desires or a favorable outcome for a particular situation. See yourself experiencing your greatest desire or favorable outcome. Take your time to fully immerse in your visualization.

Now write down the feelings that you have experienced during this visualization.

Visualization Practice

Decide what you would like to visualize. Relax your body and mind. Immerse yourself in your visualization as if you are experiencing it now. Bask in the feelings and sensations of your visualization.

Now write down the feelings that you have experienced during this visualization.

____

____

____

____

____

____

____

____

____

Visualization Practice

Decide what you would like to visualize. Relax your body and mind. Immerse yourself in your visualization as if you are experiencing it now. Bask in the feelings and sensations of your visualization.

Now write down the feelings that you have experienced during this visualization.

____

____

____

____

____

____

____

____

Visualization Practice

Decide what you would like to visualize. Relax your body and mind. Immerse yourself in your visualization as if you are experiencing it now. Bask in the feelings and sensations of your visualization.

Now write down the feelings that you have experienced during this visualization.

____

____

____

____

____

____

____

____

Visualization Practice

Decide what you would like to visualize. Relax your body and mind. Immerse yourself in your visualization as if you are experiencing it now. Bask in the feelings and sensations of your visualization.

Now write down the feelings that you have experienced during this visualization.

____

____

____

____

____

____

____

____

I am taking small
consistent steps toward
my dreams every day

I believe in my abilities
and the path I've chosen

Obstacles are just
opportunities to learn
and grow on my journey

I am committed to nurturing my passions and making them a priority

My dreams are worth pursuing, and I am worth the effort

I am open to new opportunities that align with my passions

I trust the timing of my journey; everything happens for a reason

I embrace failure as a stepping stone to success

I am creating a life that reflects my deepest passions

I find inspiration and motivation within myself every day

Action Commitment

Select one of your dreams. Reflect on one specific action, no matter how small it is, that you can commit to taking today or in the near future to move closer to that dream. Write it down.

____

____

____

____

____

____

____

____

Engage in this exercise regularly to train your brain. On page you will find more templates like this, to practice your action commitment.

Action Commitment

Select one of your dreams. Reflect on one specific action, no matter how small it is, that you can commit to taking today or in the near future to move closer to that dream. Write it down.

____

____

____

____

____

____

____

____

Engage in this exercise regularly to train your brain. On page you will find more templates like this, to practice your action commitment.

Action Commitment

Select one of your dreams. Reflect on one specific action, no matter how small it is, that you can commit to taking today or in the near future to move closer to that dream. Write it down.

____

____

____

____

____

____

____

____

Engage in this exercise regularly to train your brain. On page you will find more templates like this, to practice your action commitment.

Action Commitment

Select one of your dreams. Reflect on one specific action, no matter how small it is, that you can commit to taking today or in the near future to move closer to that dream. Write it down.

____

____

____

____

____

____

____

____

Engage in this exercise regularly to train your brain. On page you will find more templates like this, to practice your action commitment.

Action Commitment

Select one of your dreams. Reflect on one specific action, no matter how small it is, that you can commit to taking today or in the near future to move closer to that dream. Write it down.

____

____

____

____

____

____

____

____

Engage in this exercise regularly to train your brain. On page you will find more templates like this, to practice your action commitment.